the **chrome** book

WITHDRAWN

second edition

by C H Rome

chromebook.lotontech.com

Contents

About the Book

This is the much revised and expanded edition of the book "The Chrome Book" that I wrote and published in July 2011. At the time of the first edition it was early days in the Google Chromebook story, with the first dedicated Chrome-based devices – the Chromebook computers – having only just come on the market. The purpose of the first edition was to test the market for Chromebooks themselves and for my book about them.

With several new Chromebook models having been launched in the intervening time, including the compact desktop Chromebox and a new much cheaper pre-Christmas 2012 Chromebook, I felt it was about time to update and expand the content – to do the book "properly".

The title of this book, The Chrome Book, is something of a play on words. Not only is it a book about the Google-specified range of low-maintenance personal computers known as "Chromebooks", but it is also about the Chrome web browser, operating system, and server-side cloud computing ecosystem. So "The Chrome Book" is about "the Chromebooks" and everything else that goes under the "Chrome" banner – at least at a high level.

Since this book is more generally about the Chrome web browser and its role in cloud computing, some additional developments in the overall Chrome ecosystem have prompted the second edition; for example the evolution of Google Docs into Google Drive.

This book is therefore not limited to covering only the Chromebook computers. It's about the whole Google cloud computing ecosystem comprising the Chrome browser (whether it is running on a Chromebook or a PC) and the set of cloud-based Google Apps (whether running in the Chrome browser on a Chromebook, in the Chrome web browser on a PC, or even on an Android tablet or mobile phone). It's a book about how you can make the transition to cloud computing with Google as your central service provider—whatever device you're using.

Although I hint at the possibilities for introducing the Chrome cloud computing model to the corporate enterprise, this book is aimed primarily at the individual home user, freelance worker, or small business owner.

As you read through this book you may get the impression that I am some kind of Google evangelist. I suppose I am, but not "religiously" so. A few years ago I may equally have been described as a Microsoft evangelist, and I probably have an old business card somewhere that says that I once was. The fact is that I am evangelizing Google because – right now, though maybe not forever – the Google cloud computing platform comprising Google Apps, the Chrome web browser, and the Chromebook computer provides the best all round solution for my personal and business needs.

The book is arranged as follows:

In *Chapter 1 – The Case for Cloud Computing with Chrome* I briefly state the case for cloud computing, and in particular the Google Chrome model for cloud computing.

In *Chapter 2 – The Chromebook Computer* I introduce the dedicated Chromebook computers that were first announced by Google in May 2011 and which have gone through several iterations including the Chromebox desktop alternative.

In *Chapter 3 – Google Drive* I describe Google's cloud-based online file system, including how this can be used to synchronize and backup the contents of your PC hard drive.

In *Chapter 4 – Google Docs* I document the documents (pun acknowledged) and other office file types – such as spreadsheets – that you can create in your Google Drive using the provided online creation tools as an alternative to using Microsoft Office.

In *Chapter 5 – Gmail, Contacts and Calendar* I demonstrate the email and calendar facilities provided by Google.

In *Chapter 6 – Google Apps (in brief)* I briefly cover the more commercially-oriented Google Apps facilities for managing a multi-user IT infrastructure without the IT infrastructure.

In *Chapter 7 – The Chrome Web Store* I tell you how you can extend your Chrome experience by installing extensions, browser themes, and apps from the Chrome Web Store.

In *Chapter 8 – The Chrome Web Browser* I describe a few of the features of the Chrome web browser that distinguish it from other web browsers.

In *Chapter 9 – Your Google Account* I tell you how your Google Account is the central coordination point for all your Google services and storage.

In *Chapter 10 – Cloud Computing Conundrums* I alert you to some of the problems thrown up by the cloud computing model versus the traditional PC computing model; and most importantly I show you how these problems can be addressed.

In *Chapter 11 – My Head in the Clouds* I conclude by bringing you up to date on how my own transition to cloud computing with Google Chrome and the Chromebook has progressed.

About the Author

C H Rome is a pseudonym, which I have used because I think it's really clever how it spells out the word "chrome".

1 – The Case for Cloud Computing with Chrome

When Google announced on 11 May 2011 that Samsung- and Acer-manufactured Chromebook computers running the web-oriented Chrome OS would become available to buy worldwide from 15 June, the question on everyone's lips might have been:

"Why would I want one?"

In fact, this question had been on the lips of many of the world's technology watchers ever since Google announced the conception of its new web-oriented operating system some two years earlier.

If you're reading my book because you've just taken delivery of your very own Chromebook, you may already have rationalized your decision. Alternatively, you might be thinking "Oh, what have I just bought?"

Whether you're thinking about buying a Chromebook, or you've already got one, I will help you rationalize the decision you are about to make or have just made.

If you're not in the market for a Chromebook right now, you might nonetheless be thinking about moving further towards the more web-centric cloud computing model which no longer obliges you to have a top of the range PC or Mac computer. In this case, I will help you rationalize your journey into the cloud, which requires only a web browser (ideally Google Chrome) running on your Linux netbook, Android phone or tablet, Apple Mac, or even, your existing PC. In fact, the beauty of Chrome and the associated Google ecosystem is that you can begin your cloud computing journey without buying a new device at all. For several months before acquiring a 'proper' Chromebook I operated as much as possible in pseudo-cloud mode: interacting only with web sites using my Windows PC and a laptop computer running a pre-release version of the Chromium operating system.

Your Head in the Clouds

How do you spend most of your time on your computer? I bet most of your time is spent shopping online, banking online, booking hotels, emailing, Googling for information, and (for many of you) networking with your friends on Facebook. None of these activities requires a fully functional traditional PC but all of them depend on your Internet connection. If this is all you do then all you really need is a cheap and cheerful device that acts as the window to your online world. And that's why you need a Chromebook.

Okay, so you also write documents and manage spreadsheets which require the full power of the Microsoft Office suite. Or do they? Have you checked out what the free-to-use web-based Google Docs office suite can do recently? I know you think that web-based applications are no substitute for 'proper' applications installed on your PC, but didn't you once think that Microsoft Outlook was an irreplaceable PC application for your email, calendar and contacts? If you're like me, nowadays you probably manage all your emails and calendar via a web interface like Google's Gmail or Yahoo! Mail and their associated calendar and contacts web applications.

Welcome to the world of cloud computing, where you do everything and store everything online.

Welcome to a world where you no longer need to worry about backing up your important files or keeping your virus checker up-to-date. It's all done for you. Providing you trust Google, that is.

Welcome to a world where you no longer need to synchronize your mobile phone and PC; where with a complementary Android phone you can keep your email, calendar, contacts and documents perfectly in sync automatically over-the-airwaves simply by putting Google at the centre of your online world.

The other major technology companies including Microsoft and Apple also have their own cloud computing strategies and platforms, for example Apple's iCloud service that will make sure everything is synchronized between your various Apple devices. This may be a serious contender for Apple aficionados. Microsoft would once have been the natural choice for my own venture into the cloud, but I find their Microsoft Office web apps to be too restrictive for my needs because they pretty much necessitate you owning the fully-licensed locally-installed versions anyway. I guess Microsoft has too much investment in PC-based operating systems and office applications to see them die anytime soon. So for me, for now, it's Google all the way.

The World Wide Workforce

So much for the individual perspective on cloud computing, but what about the business perspective? The business case for cloud computing may be even stronger.

Why equip every one of your employees with an overpowered and overpriced PC or Mac when most if not all of their tasks involve interacting with web applications provided via the Internet or your company intranet? Wouldn't a simpler desktop or in-the-field terminal – rather like the old mainframe green screen terminals, but now in full Technicolor – be more appropriate? And just think about how much money you could save by not employing armies of technical staff to keep all of those traditional PCs and Macs up-to-date and virus free.

It's been done before with mainframe computing. It's been tried before with the never-widely-adopted Sun Microsystems 'JavaStation' terminals that aimed to reduce total cost of ownership (TCO) to near zero. But what makes it truly possible this time around is the ubiquity of broadband Internet access.

In fact, your company may already be doing it. Using technologies like Citrix, many companies have for some time been allowing their staff to run office applications like Microsoft Word on their remotely-connected laptop or desktop PCs without actually having the Microsoft Office suite installed on those machines. The software runs on the server computers back at base, and any field computer merely provides a window on the remote computing session. This kind of company cloud computing lessens the burden of installing and configuring the software individually on numerous client computers, and it fits neatly with the Chromebook philosophy of having no software -- well, not much of it -- installed locally.

I bet you've heard numerous scandal stories about government, military, and commercial laptops containing sensitive data having been left on trains. With Chromebooks there is no such danger, because you will lose only the laptop and not the sensitive information it contains. The idea is that hardly anything is stored locally, and anything that is – including temporary Internet files – is encrypted.

In terms of enabling the worldwide workforce, Google instigated Chromebooks for Business and Chromebooks for Education programs to 'rent' Chromebooks to businesses and educational establishments for between $20 (education) and $28 (business) per month. When you consider that this would have made the $429 Samsung Series 5 Chromebook cost twice as much over the 36-month minimum term it sounds expensive; but when you consider that you can dramatically cut your IT support costs, and effectively outsource the rest to Google for the all-inclusive price, it begins to sound much more reasonable.

Companies that have piloted the use of Chromebooks in their organizations have included American Airlines, Intercontinental Hotels Group, Groupon, Logitech, Konica Minolta, National Geographic, and Virgin America.

The Case for the Chromebox

In the first half of 2012, Google released the "Chromebox" desktop equivalent of the "Chromebook" netbook or laptop. Attach this compact unit to your TV screen or dedicated display unit, attach a proper keyboard and mouse to it, and you have a relatively inexpensive and efficient way to browse the web and work in the cloud.

The case for the Chromebox may be even greater than the case for the Chromebook, because both of them need an almost-permanent Internet connection, and your desktop-replacement Chromebox will almost certainly always be within range of a Wifi signal in your home or at work. Having said this, the desktop-replacement Chromebox is so portable that it is possible to pick it up and carry it around, and plug it into someone else's screen wherever you go.

People Don't Pay for Efficiency

The preceding arguments in favor of cloud computing sound pretty convincing, so why might some people be reluctant to choose the Chromebook computer for the user end of cloud computing? It's because no one likes to pay more for less; or to put it another way: no one likes to pay for 'efficiency'.

I discovered a while ago that in business people are reluctant to pay for efficiency. Suppose one of my competitors quoted a client $1000 for a job to be completed in four days. Suppose I quoted $750 for the same job to be completed in two days. Guess who the client would choose to do the job?

That's right, not me!

For some deep-rooted psychological reason, some people really are reluctant to pay for efficiency.

The way I see it: my potential client could get the job done 50% sooner and 25% cheaper.

The way my potential client sees it: my 'rush job' must be more shoddy and they'd be paying me 50% more pro-rata (i.e. $375-per day vs. $250-per-day) for my time. They would rather see me providing apparently more service by spending more hours on their job.

Google faced the same problem. For the price of a Chromebook you could buy a reasonably well-specified laptop PC that does everything a Chromebook does (i.e. running the Chrome web browser) and so much more. Never mind the fact that the Chromebook boots up quicker, runs faster, and requires no explicit software updates or virus protection. On the face of it, you're getting 'less bang for your buck'. Having said this, the Chromebooks are aimed at the netbook market rather than the laptop market -- despite the larger size -- and many early commentators have said that the Chromebook is what the netbook always should have been. In this context it is worth noting that some netbooks with similar specifications were similarly priced.

Since I wrote these paragraphs in the first edition of this book, a couple of things have happened:

1. Wintel (i.e. Windows and Intel) powered "ultrabooks" have come to market, which promise the same kinds of boot-up times and sleek appearance as the Chromebooks; with price tags that now actually make Chromebooks look inexpensive in comparison

2. In October 2012, Samsung launched a significantly less expensive ARM-powered Chromebook, which at the time of writing seems to be selling well and which as a knock-on effect appears to have triggered a reduction in the prices of the existing Chromebook models.

A Personal Anecdote

As the neighborhood 'IT expert' I am often called upon to diagnose friends' and families' PC problems... even though my background is in business and systems analysis rather than PC support. To be honest, I hate it. I hate being presented with a plethora of hardware and software compatibility issues when my clients (who don't actually pay me) are really just looking for a simple way to get online. Sometimes I despair at how personal computers are sold to the general public as though they are consumer items. But consumer items, they are not. When you switch on your TV, you expect it simply to work without having to read the whole manual or attend a 'TV for Beginners' course before tuning into your favorite soap opera. With personal computers it's not so straightforward, as I'm sure you already know. But Google's new Chromebook initiative might just change that.

Summary

In this chapter I have addressed such issues as why you would want to adopt the cloud computing model (and buy a Chromebook computer) at all. I have highlighted the fact that you probably do most if not all of your "computing" within a web browser, such that the transition to cloud computing is not such a big step. From a corporate perspective, I have suggested that cloud computing with Chrome might be an enabler for the worldwide workforce.

I concluded by explaining why some people were initially hesitant about Chromebook computers – because no one likes to pay for efficiency, whatever they tell you – and I related my personal anecdote about why this new world of cloud computing with Chrome could make my own life easier.

Ready, Steady...

Are you ready to put not just your head in the cloud, but your whole life in the clouds? To have all of your data stored securely (we hope) in a Google data center, so that you can access it anytime from anywhere using lightweight and low-cost devices such as the Chromebook and Chromebox? Will you be able to find web-based alternatives to the myriad software programs you have installed locally on your PC?

Let's find out.

2 – The Chromebook Computer

This chapter is about Google's low-maintenance web-centric "Chromebook" computers. If you're thinking about purchasing a Chromebook, or you've just taken delivery of one, read on. If you don't have a Chromebook, and don't intend to get one, you can skip ahead to the subsequent chapters that explain aspects of the Chrome web browser and the Google cloud computing ecosystem regardless of whether you are operating on a Chromebook or a traditional PC.

The Advent of Chrome Computing

Google first announced the development of a new lightweight Chrome OS operating system, to be targeted initially at netbook computers, in July 2009. Two years later the first fruits of those labors came to fruition in the form of the Chromebook computers: netbook computers in all but name, which run Chrome OS rather than the traditional Microsoft Windows. Although the first batches of Chromebooks looked superficially like laptop computers, they had been designed from the ground up to behave differently and to solve many of the problems associated with the traditional laptop.

In a summary those key features were (and are):

Always Connected

Unlike a traditional PC where you log into the computer and then separately connect to the Internet, when you log into a Chromebook it establishes a Wifi or 3G connection immediately. So you're online straightaway, you stay online, and you don't have to wrestle with network connection settings.

Instant Web

The Chromebook boots up from cold start much faster than a traditional PC (in about 10 seconds). But unlike a traditional PC, you will rarely shut it down. Just like when using your mobile phone, you will most likely put your Chromebook into standby mode and watch it resume instantly. The optimized Chrome browser loads web pages quickly and (unlike some popular tablet computers) fully supports Adobe Flash web sites.

Same Experience Everywhere

You interact mainly with web sites, not with installed programs. Little or nothing is stored locally on the Chromebook computer, and all your documents and settings are stored centrally in 'the cloud'. You don't need to worry about backing up your programs or data, and if you lose your Chromebook you can quickly connect to the same online experience using another one.

Friends Let Friends Log In

You can log into your web experience using a friend's Chromebook, or they can log into their web experience using yours, and the Chrome browser automatically reconfigures the settings, apps, and extensions to whoever is logged in. Everything is kept private, and you can optionally allow guests to browse the web without really logging in at all.

Web Apps

Your mobile phone has apps, your tablet device has apps, and your Chromebook computer has web apps that you can discover in the Chrome Web Store. You don't "install" the majority of these web apps as such; you simply run them straight from the web, and thanks to HTML 5 some of them don't grind to a complete halt if your Internet connection goes down. But don't forget the existing web sites you use, which run just as well on the Chromebook as ever they did.

Security Built-In

With little or no software installed locally apart from a few optional browser extensions, there is little or no danger from viruses and malware. The security of your operating environment now becomes Google's problem, not yours.

Forever Fresh

You won't be receiving any operating system or software update CDs or DVDs. All of this is done automatically over the air (OTA) behind the scenes; so your Chromebook will always be bang up to date and you can carry on computing.

Better Battery Life

If you've been used to getting just 2-4 hours of life out of your laptop between battery charges, you'll be pleasantly surprised by the better battery life that your Chromebook provides.

Who Needs a Chromebook Computer?

Here are a few of the members of the Chromebook target audience (and those who are not):

- Tina is a student living away from home. She likes to socialize via Facebook, email the folks back home, and write the occasional essay for her classes. Her university provides free Wifi access to its students. The Chromebook is for her.

- Tim wants to get his elderly parents online without the burden of resolving installation conflicts and keeping antivirus software up to date. He merely wants to provide them with a 'window on the web' and a proper keyboard, so the Chromebook is for him... or them.

- Terry is a freelance journalist who researches topics and submits articles to magazine editors, and who otherwise spends his time reading the news and managing his money online. The Chromebook is for him.

- Tracey runs a real estate office. Her staff need to take pictures of properties and write descriptions while out in the field, and publish these to the web before even returning to the office. Tracey has a very limited budget for IT support, so a team set of Chromebooks may be suitable for her and her staff.

- Toby is a trendy 'man about town' who puts style before substance and who likes to show off his cool-brand gadgets to his friends; even though he doesn't use those gadgets to even half their potential. The Chromebook is probably not for him.

- Trisha is a games developer who writes code using a special PC-based software development kit. Her media rich creations necessitate the use of a top-of-the-range video and audio editing software suite. The Chromebook is not for her.

A Personal Note

When you've been using a Chromebook for a little while you'll find yourself loving the almost-instant switch on, extra-long battery life, and low noise (due to no moving parts) a lot more than you might think. I know I do!

The Operating System

In any other book about a computer you would expect to find a section or chapter telling you about the operating system: the installed system software that basically 'runs' the computer. For PCs, think Microsoft Windows or Linux. For Apple Macs, think MAC OS X. For the Apple iPad, think iOS. And for Android phones, think - well - Android.

In this book there will be no such discussion of the operating system as such because, from the user's perspective at least, the web browser is the operating system. With a few necessary exceptions, the only program you run on the Chromebook is the Chrome web browser. And when you run the web apps in the web browser, most of the processing takes place on a server computer at the other end of your Internet connection. With few programs running locally on your Chromebook, the local operating system (okay, so there is one really, but only true geeks need to know about it) has very little to do apart from running the web browser and controlling the screen, keyboard, Wifi connection, and USB ports.

The Chromebook Computers

I should say at the outset that all Chromebooks should offer essentially the same experience; the differences between them being mainly cosmetic (how nice they look), a matter of performance (how much memory and what speed processor they have), and format (whether they look like traditional laptops or like the alternative Chromebox).

The first two Chromebooks out of the starting blocks in mid-2011 were the Samsung Series 5 and the Acer AC700. These were followed by the Samsung Series 5 550 and the Samsung "Chromebox" — which resembles a very compact desktop computer, and which you plug into your television screen or dedicated monitor.

In October 2012, Samsung launched (and Google promoted) a new less-expensive Chromebook, which should help address previous criticisms that you could do everything that a Chromebook can do – and more – using an inexpensive traditional laptop. Those criticisms missed the point of the Chromebook concept, but they did make people think twice about shelling out what looked like more money for less functionality.

It is the new hot-off-the-press (at the time of writing) less expensive Chromebook that is used as the demonstration vehicle in this book; but it shouldn't really matter which one you're using... or intend to use.

What's in the Box?

It may differ depending on which Chromebook (or Chromebox) you buy, and when you buy it, but the box for the October 2012 edition Samsung Chromebook contained just two items: the computer and a power supply.

There were no installation CDs or DVDs, because they're simply not needed. The whole point is that you're not allowed to install your own software apart from Chrome web apps and browser extensions, and the Chrome OS itself will be updated automatically over the

Internet at periodic intervals. It is in this way that the Chromebook is designed to remain low-maintenance and virus-free.

To be fair, the box also contains a few flimsy booklets, but no comprehensive "manual" – just like most computers these days. The idea is for you to access the Chromebook's own built-in and on-line help… and to get extra assistance from books like the one you're reading now.

Accessing the built-in Chrome OS help is as easy as this:

The Chromebook Initial Setup

When setting up your Chromebook for the first time, the first thing you need to do is…

23

Get Connected

The first time you fire up your Chromebook – merely by opening the lid – you will be presented with a dialog asking you to **Select your language**, **Select your keyboard**, and **Select a network**. The Chromebook is designed to be "always connected" so it makes sense to select a network before you do anything else.

The list of networks you are presented with will depend on whether you have a Wifi-only or 3G+Wifi Chromebook. I'm running a Wifi Chromebook for demonstration purposes, so I am presented with the following Wifi networks from which to choose:

- **LOTONtech** (the name of my company Wifi network)

- **BTFON** (the public network presented by my British Telecom router)

- **OliWifi** (which must be my neighbor's Wifi network)

Actually, I am presented with an additional network named **Ethernet**. This is because I attached my Android phone to the Chromebook via a USB cable and enabled the **USB Tethering** option on the phone. It means I can connect my Chromebook to the Internet via the Android phone's 3G signal.

Check for Updates

Once your Chromebook is connected to a network, you will likely find that it checks for and installs updates. The idea is that the Chromebook is automatically kept always up-to-date with the latest Chrome OS operating system, without you having to manually download and install updates or purchase operating system installation CDs or DVDs.

One thing to keep in mind is that the client portion of the Chrome OS – i.e. that which is installed on your Chromebook itself – is in any case intended to be small and light, consisting of the Chrome web browser and not much else. The majority of the "apps" you will run will be in the form of repackaged web sites where most of the processing takes place at the other end of your Internet connection.

Sign In

Once connected to a network, you will be asked to **Sign in** to your Google Account if you have one, or to **Create a Google Account** if you don't.

You also have a third option to not sign in at all, and to **Browse as a Guest**. This option is useful if you or a friend simply want to browse the web without associating your activity with a particular Google Account. Note, though, that settings won't be saved when you browse as a guest, and each time will be an entirely new experience. If you browse as a guest the first time after entering your Wifi network password or key, don't be surprised if you're asked for that same network password or key the next time you log in.

The first time you log in using a Google Account, you will be prompted to choose a picture to appear for your account on the Chromebook sign-in screen. You can choose from one of the default pictures, your Google+ profile picture, or a picture of yourself staring into the Chromebook's webcam.

Whenever you power up the Chromebook in future – and assuming other family members, friends or work colleagues have used your Chromebook (which is all part of the plan) – then you will be presented with a sign-in screen that allows you to choose which identity (i.e. Google Account holder) to log in as; or to **+ Add user** for one of those friends, family, or colleagues.

Interacting with the Chromebook

You will interact with your Chromebook using the keyboard and touchpad, and by manipulating items on the screen. Here's how...

Power On / Power Off

Think of your Chromebook as more like your mobile phone, which goes from powered-on to standby (and back again) pretty much instantaneously. Just close the Chromebook lid to switch off the screen and go into standby mode, and then flip it open again to resume working immediately.

Note that by default the Chromebook will resume without requiring a password, which means that anyone could use it simply by lifting the lid. For greater security you can change one of the **Users** settings, as shown below, to "**Require password to wake from sleep**".

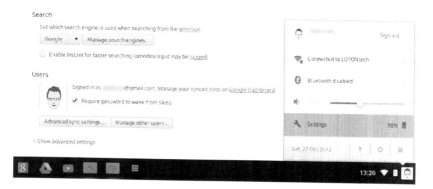

You can also lock your user account at any time without closing the lid, so that a password is required to resume, by pressing the **Power** button at the top-right of the keyboard for one second. Pressing the power button for a few seconds shuts down the chromebook completely, and you can power it up again either by pressing the power button once more or by lifting the lid (if you had closed it).

Chromebook Keyboard

As you can see below, the Chromebook keyboard is a regular QWERTY keyboard with the PC "function keys" (F1-F12) on the top row replaced by some dedicated Chromebook keys.

The second and third left and right arrow keys act as shortcut keys for the Chrome browser's *forward* and *back* functions, and the fourth key acts as a shortcut for the browser's *refresh* (or reload) function.

The fourth key acts as a shortcut key for maximizing (making full-screen) whichever browser window you are working in; and the fifth key allows you to switch between browser windows when you have more than one of them open – and it's particularly useful when they are all maximized.

Note that in addition to the dedicated function keys, there are also key combinations that perform specific tasks, for example:

- Pressing the **ctrl** and **m** keys together (**ctrl** + **m**) launches the file manager.

- Pressing the **ctrl** and *switch window* key (sixth key on the top row) together captures a screenshot of what is currently displayed on the Chromebook screen, and saves it as a Portable Network Graphics (.png) image in your Downloads folder.

Chromebook Touchpad

You can plug a USB mouse into one of the USB sockets of your Chromebook, and in the case of a Chromebox you will have to, but the Chromebook also has a touchpad at the front of the keyboard which allows you to move the mouse cursor around the screen.

Gliding your finger around the pad moves the mouse cursor, and lightly tapping the pad (or pressing for a more responsive 'click') is equivalent to making a selection by clicking the left mouse button on a traditional mouse. A right-button click – which usually displays a context menu of additional options – is performed by tapping or pressing on the touchpad with two fingers.

The Desktop, Windows, Tabs and Apps

In early versions of the Chrome OS, the screen would show a full-screen web browser... and that was it. The Chrome OS user interface has now evolved to resemble a PC desktop-style display; albeit one that can only really display different browser windows:

TABS   New Window

WINDOWS

FAVOURITE APPS

The screenshot above shows the distinction between WINDOWS and TABS. Theoretically you could run separate web apps and display separate web pages using multiple tabs within a single browser window, but I find it useful to have 'batches' of tabs running in different browser windows. For example: I might use multiple tabs within one browser window for my Google email and calendar, and use multiple tabs within another browser window for the on-line newspaper pages I'm reading. When running these browser windows maximized (click the square icons at the top-right of the windows) I can easily switch between my Google browser window and my 'news' browser window by pressing the *switch windows* key.

Across the bottom of the Chrome desktop you will find a horizontal bar to which you can 'pin' your favorite web apps, and you can see the full list of your apps by selecting the checkerboard icon. This may be reminiscent of the user interface on your Android smartphone, or you can think of it as like the Windows 7 Start Menu.

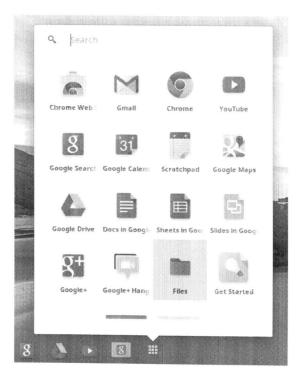

Some of the available apps are merely existing web sites that are accessible via these 'app' shortcuts; and that's the whole point about the Chrome OS – to access most if not all apps via the Chrome web browser when connected to the Internet.

Some of the available apps are locally-installed 'off-line' apps that will operate even in the absence of an Internet connection. In the previous screenshot I have highlighted the **Files** app for special attention.

The File Manager

You can launch the Chrome OS file manager by selecting the **Files** app icon as shown above, or by pressing the shortcut key combination **ctrl+m**. In this file manager window you will see the available data drives or file storage locations listed in the left-hand column, which will typically include your **Downloads** folder (where documents will be placed when downloaded from the World Wide Web), your **Google Drive** (which is the online storage linked to your Google Account), and any external drives such as a USB stick or SD card that you have inserted into one of the Chromebook or Chromebox USB sockets.

In the following screenshot I have launched a file manager window to view my **Downloads** (as thumbnails) and a separate file manager window to view the contents of my **Google Drive** (in list view).

You can move files from one location to another, for example from your USB drive or SD card to your Google Drive... and vice versa. In this case you might right-click (or two-finger tap) the required file to launch its context menu and choose the **Copy** option, and then browse to a folder in the other location before right-clicking again and choosing the **Paste** option to deposit the file at its destination.

Opening Media Files

The Chromebook has a basic multimedia player that allows you to play songs and movies from the file manager, whether these are on an inserted USB stick or SD card or have been downloaded to your

Downloads folder. You don't need to be connected to the Internet in order to play these media files.

There is also a basic image editor that allows you to perform simple functions like cropping an image, changing its brightness, or rotating left or right. To edit an image, just open it via the file manager and click the pencil (**Edit**) icon at the bottom-right of the screen.

Before you edit an image in any way, take notice of the warning message that states "**Your edits are saved automatically**" and the check box labeled **Overwrite original**. If you want the original image to remain unchanged, you *must* uncheck this box before cropping, brightening or rotating!

Multiple Chromebook Users

Note that unless you expressly forbid it, anyone with a Google Account can log in via your Chromebook. It's nothing to worry about, and all part of the plan, because the whole point is that (theoretically, at least) anyone can access their Google account, apps and settings via any Chrome device anywhere. Which includes you, if you happen to lose your Chromebook or its gets damaged, in which case you can get up-and-running again really quickly by finding a friend with a Chromebook or by going out and buying another one. It's not like the old days when, if you lost or damaged your PC, you'd have lost all of the files and programs stored on it.

Summary

In this chapter I have described some of the key features of the Chromebook concept, and suggested what kinds of people might be interested in a Chromebook computer. I have described what a Chromebook is, how you sign in to it and how you interact with it via the keyboard and screen. I have also described how to move files between the built-in storage, any plugged-in storage (such as a USB stick or SD card), and the Google Drive that will be introduced more formally in a later chapter.

the
chrome
book

3 – Google Drive

In the cloud computing model, all of your documents and other files are stored "in the cloud" on a server computer at the other end of your Internet connection rather than being stored locally on your PC hard drive. The idea is that you can access your files anytime from anywhere using any device that has an Internet connection and which (in the Google case) runs the Chrome web browser.

In the Google cloud computing world, the home to your files on the Internet is the Google Drive that is associated with your Google Account.

Navigating the Google Drive

You can access your Google Drive by clicking the **Drive** option on your Google account menu bar displayed at the top of the web browser when you're in Gmail or Google Calendar, or you can click the triangular Google Drive app icon, or you can simply type **drive.google.com** into the Chrome web browser's address bar.

As shown in the next figure, you can navigate your Google Drive folders in the left-hand column and see the contents of the currently-selected folder (called a **Collection**) to the right – which is very much the same as when operating a local file explorer such as Windows Explorer, except that this file explorer is on the web. In this example I have selected a **Collection** named **Business** which contains a Google spreadsheet named **Test Spreadsheet** (imaginative, eh?) and a sub-collection named **NOTES**.

You can use the **CREATE** button, or right-click a specific folder, in order to create a new file—which might be a **Document**, **Presentation**, **Spreadsheet**, **Form**, **Drawing** or **Collection**. Note that the documents, presentations and spreadsheets that you create here will be in Google's own web-based format rather than (for example) in Microsoft Office format; but it is possible to export to and import from the Microsoft Office equivalent formats. Further guidance on creating and editing these Google Docs files is given in the next chapter.

When using the web-based Google Drive you can perform the kinds of file manipulation tasks that you are used to—for example, dragging files from one folder to another or renaming files (by right-clicking and choosing **Rename** from the pop-up context menu).

Using the Google Drive to Store Non-Google Files

Just like Microsoft's rival SkyDrive, you can use your Google Drive to store or backup any or all of your files on the web, even if they're not Google documents or spreadsheets.

To upload a file to your Google Drive, all you need to do is click the upload icon shown circled in the following screenshot and then select the required file from the PC or Chromebook file system (e.g. your Chromebook **Downloads** folder or an attached USB stick). Be sure to have selected the required Google Drive destination folder / collection first.

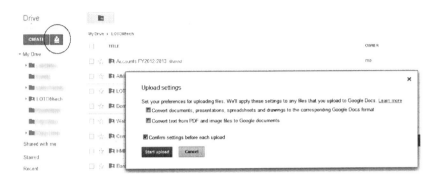

As shown above, when you upload a non-Google file to your Google Drive you are given the option to convert the file to a corresponding Google Docs format file (if there is one) — for example to convert a Microsoft Word document to a Google Docs document. As a general rule, I tend to upload without conversion so that the file is kept as-is and is merely *stored* on my Google Drive.

Accessing Your Google Drive

You can access your web-based Google Drive from any computer or other device that runs a web browser – ideally Google Chrome – but on specific devices such as the Chromebook (or Chromebox) and your Windows PC there are other ways of interacting with the Google Drive.

Google Drive on Your Chromebook

You can access your Google Drive on the web via your Chromebook either by typing **drive.google.com** into a browser tab or by selecting the **Google Drive** app icon as shown in the previous chapter.

You can also access your Google Drive on your Chromebook via the **Files** app as shown in the previous chapter, which provides a convenient way for you to copy files such as pictures and other non-Google files to your online Google Drive from another source such as a USB stick or from your Downloads folder.

Note that when you access your Google Drive via the file manager, you will not automatically be able to open a file from your Google Drive when you are offline unless (when online) you have first checked the box to make the file **Available offline**—unless, of course, the file originated on your Chromebook in the first place. In the following screenshot see how I have made one picture file **Available offline** (so I can open it on my Chromebook even when disconnected) and how another picture file that I uploaded from another device is not flagged as **Available offline** (so I receive an error message when trying to open it on this Chromebook).

The plot thickens. In the following figure you can see that when attempting to open a Google Docs (.gdoc) document via the Chromebook file manager, I receive an error message that "**You must be online to access this file**"...

..and yet, when I access exactly the same document via the Chromebook web browser I find that it is correctly flagged as being available **Offline** (see picture below) such that I have no problems opening it in the Google Drive's "offline" mode discussed later in this chapter.

Don't worry if this is a little confusing – it is for me, too – but you get used to it after a while. At this point I just wanted to make you aware that accessing your Google Drive via the Chromebook **Files** app is not exactly equivalent to accessing your Google Drive via the Chrome web browser.

Google Drive on Your PC

I've already told you that you can use your online Google Drive to store any of your data files; and these files might be Microsoft Office files such as Word documents or Excel spreadsheets.

It can be a bit of a pain uploading these files to your Google Drive via the web interface, so Google have provided an easier way for you to synchronize your Windows PC file system with the Google Drive online storage.

Download and Configure Google Drive

You can **Download Google Drive** to your Windows PC by clicking the link shown below, which should appear in the left column of your online Google Drive.

▸ My Drive

Shared with me

Starred

Recent

More ▾

Download Google Drive

Once you've downloaded and installed the program, you can configure it to synchronize any or all of your Google Drive folders with your PC. You will also be able to change the synchronize settings at any time by right-clicking the triangular Google Drive icon on the Windows taskbar and selecting **Preferences** from the pop-up menu as shown below.

Scanning web...

Pause

Open Google Drive folder

Visit Google Drive on the web

View items shared with me

@gmail.com

11.33GB (45%) of 25.00GB used

Get more storage

Preferences...

Help

About

Quit Google Drive

Choosing which folders to synchronize is important, because the contents of your chosen folders will be downloaded to your PC— which will take both time and bandwidth. You might want to synchronize a folder containing the document(s) you are currently working on, but not the folder containing your lifetime collection of photographs.

Using Google Drive on Your PC

As part of the installation and configuration you will have chosen the location of a new Google Drive folder on your PC hard disk, and you can access this Google Drive folder via the Windows File Explorer... like this:

This provides a very convenient way of backing up your important files on the web. Just copy your Microsoft Office document files or other files to the Google Drive folder, or save them directly there, and you will see them magically copied to your online Google Drive for safe keeping. It's a lot easier than burning backup DVDs and finding a safe place to store them, isn't it?

Personally, I would be using this facility even if I didn't own a Chromebook; to ensure that my important PC files were automatically "backed up" online. In this respect I tend to regard the Google Drive folder of my PC hard drive as my entire hard drive as far as my data files are concerned, and I ignore the rest of my PC hard drive except as some to install software.

The Microsoft Word Auto-Save Problem

It may be just me, but at one point I ran into a problem when the Google Drive program was set to run all the time on my PC. The problem was that some of my Microsoft Word files became 'unsyncable', which I put down to the fact that Word was trying to auto-save my work at the same time that Google Drive was trying to sync it to the cloud.

To resolve this problem, I tend to have the Google Drive program switched off on my PC while editing Microsoft Word documents, and I run the Google Drive program manually at regular intervals – at least once per day – to back up the Word documents and other files that I have saved to my Google Drive folder. It's still much easier than the old method of backing up the important documents on my PC by burning CDs or DVDs.

Google Drive on Mac, iPhone / iPad, and Android

In addition to using Google Drive via the web and on your Windows PC or Chromebook, it is also possible to install Google Drive on your Mac computer, on your iPhone / iPad, or on your Android mobile phone or tablet.

I'm not a user of Apple products, so I can't offer any assistance with the Mac version of Google Drive which I assume operates rather like the Windows PC version. Similarly, I can't help you with the iPhone / iPad version, but I am able to tell you something about the Android mobile phone version.

In the following screenshot I am showing two things in one. I'm showing the files and folders visible via the Google Drive app on my Android mobile phone, and I'm also showing how a screenshot of this (taken on the phone itself) can itself be copied just like any other file by tapping the triangular Google Drive icon that you can see at the top-right of the picture. I use this facility all the time to get photos from my phone camera onto my Google Drive for safe storage at the tap of a button.

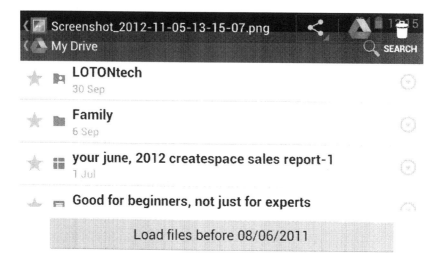

When operating Google Drive on your Android phone you can make files available offline on a one-by-one basis so that your entire online archive does not eat up all of your phone's memory; which brings us to…

Offline Docs

One of the issues with the original web-based Google Docs office suite was the fact that you had to be online in order to edit your documents. No Internet connection on your Chromebook meant that you had no access to your documents; and a lost Internet connection while editing a document meant that your changes would be lost. Google has gone some way to addressing this limitation by creating an Offline Docs facility.

In the Chrome browser, scroll down the left-hand column and expand the "**More**" item to reveal the **Offline Docs** option as shown in the screenshot below. If you see a message stating "**Now syncing Google documents for offline editing and Google spreadsheets for offline viewing.**" then you'll know that your Chromebook is all set for viewing and editing documents offline.

On another device such as your desktop or laptop Windows PC you'll have to **Enable Offline Docs** and **Install the Drive Chrome web app** on the device, as shown here:

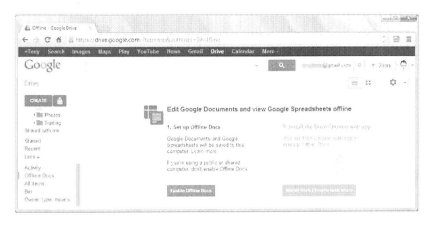

IMPORTANT NOTE: Only enable Offline Docs on your own personal computer, and not on a public or shared computer! You don't want those documents to be accessible to anyone else in your local library or Internet café.

Once the Offline Docs feature is enabled, you should see an Offline indicator next to your Google Docs files (see the example "Download Links" document below) to show that they are available for editing or viewing offline.

		OWNER	LAST MODIFI...
	TITLE		
☐ ☆ 📄 PDF Shared		me	26 Jun Tony LC
☐ ☆ 📒 Download Links Shared Offline		me	15 Jun me

My Drive ▸ LOTONtech ▸ LOTONtech Downloads

Whenever you access your Google Drive via the Chrome web browser via the triangular Google Drive app icon or simply by visiting **drive.google.com**, you will be able to edit your Google documents (or view your Google spreadsheets) whether you are online or offline. It should be pretty seamless because the Chrome web browser will detect whether or not you have an Internet connection, and will put you into online or offline mode as appropriate. Any changes that you make offline will be synced to your online Google Drive when your Internet connection is restored.

Only Applies to Google Docs

Note that this Offline Docs feature only applies to your Google-format documents. If you've downloaded the Google Drive software to sync your saved files to and from the cloud for safe keeping, you can always edit your regular Microsoft Word documents (or Excel spreadsheets, or anything else) on your PC and have them backed automatically via Google Drive when you're next connected to the Internet.

Note also that at the time of writing, only Google Docs documents are fully editable offline. Your Google spreadsheets can be viewed offline, but not edited.

Google Drive Anomalies

There are two ways to access your Google Drive:

- By clicking the triangular Google Drive app icon or visiting **drive.google.com** in the Chrome web browser on your Chromebook or PC.

- By navigating to the Google Drive folder on your PC or by launching the Files app on your Chromebook.

These two ways of accessing your Google Drive are not exactly equivalent, and you might notice some anomalies.

For example, at the time of writing I have found that I cannot access the Offline Docs versions of my documents via the Files app on my Chromebook. When not connected to the Internet, the Google Docs listed in the Chromebook file manager are grayed-out, and attempting to open one of them results in the message "You are offline – You must be online to access this file." Yet I can open the same file in offline mode by visiting **drive.google.com** in the Chromebook web browser or by double-clicking the file shortcut in the Google Drive folder of my PC file manager.

Once you get used to this kind of anomaly – and it's probably not the only one – it becomes easy enough to work with your Google Drive documents... online and offline.

Summary

In this chapter I have introduced the Google Drive cloud-based online storage; how you navigate it and how you can use it to create and arrange the Google-format documents and presentations that will be described in more detail in the next chapter. I have also explained how you can use Google Drive to store or back-up your non-Google files such as Microsoft Office documents, and in this context I have explained how Google Drive interoperates with the local file system of your Chromebook, PC, Android mobile phone or other device.

4 – Google Docs

In the previous chapter I told you about the Google Drive, and how it is possible to use the web interface to create new Google-format documents, spreadsheets, presentations and other files in your drive. This ability to create and edit various "office" (with a small "o", not Microsoft Office) documents is what used to be known as Google Docs—before they changed the name of the whole shebang to Google Drive.

In this chapter I'll dig a little deeper into what might be described as the Google "office suite". It's the office suite that you'll be using by default on your web-only Chromebook, but it's not the only option as you will discover towards the end of the chapter.

Document

The first and most useful office file type that you can create in your Google Drive using Google Docs is the "Google Doc"...or Document. As a freelance writer for several publications, I have written numerous structured (i.e. with headings) feature articles, and shared the end results with editors directly via the web, without going anywhere near Microsoft Word. I even wrote the first edition of this book as a Google Document.

Will Google Docs Suit Your Needs (and Mine)?

As an e-book creation tool, the Google Docs work processor is perfectly acceptable. As a tool for writing linear articles with alternating text and pictures, it is perfectly acceptable. But as a tool for producing professionally formatted book manuscripts and converting these to print-ready Portable Document Format (PDF) files for publication in paperback format, it is not up to the job... yet.

As a professional publisher of books, I do still sometimes need the very advanced features of Microsoft Word when typesetting manuscripts for publication; but in the previous chapter I showed how Word can co-exist with Google Drive, and in *Chapter 10 – Cloud Computing Conundrums* I will show how I can run Microsoft Word (kind-of) on my Chromebook.

Typically it means that I can spend perhaps 80% of my time "in the cloud" writing a base manuscript and benefiting from the automatic backups; but I have to come out of the cloud for the remaining 20% of the time to "finish off" using Microsoft Word or another more comprehensive tool. It's easy enough to do because Google Docs allows me to export my almost-complete manuscript in the widely interchangeable Microsoft Word (.doc) format.

What Can Google Docs Do for You?

Having set your expectations at a suitably low level; let me now tell you what you can achieve with a Google Docs document. I wrote the first edition of this book as a Google Document, and for e-books I can tell you that it works pretty well. As proof, the following figure shows a section of the original book manuscript (as a Google Document) comprising a styled heading followed by alternating text and graphics. You can also see in this figure how one of my colleagues has commented on the document using the collaboration features of Google Docs that will be discussed shortly.

Even though *you* may have moved to the cloud, not everyone else will have done so just yet, so some people – like the magazine editors with whom I work – will still be expecting you to provide them with documents in Microsoft Word format. You can convert any Google Docs document in Microsoft Word (.doc) format and other popular formats such as Portable Document Format (.pdf) by choosing **Download as** from the **File** menu.

Presentation

You can create presentations using Google Docs as an alternative to creating them using Microsoft Powerpoint, but don't (yet) expect to be able to do all of the things that PowerPoint allows you to do such as having complete control over the size and orientation of your slides. Also be aware that if you upload existing Powerpoint presentations to Google Docs, something will be lost in the translation.

With the bad news out of the way, let me tell you the good news.

The idea of creating presentations 'in the cloud' is a perfectly sound idea. Most presentations are created to be taken somewhere for showing, usually to another company. Some presenters have found themselves in the unfortunate position of having somehow lost, while traveling, the USB drive, DVD, or even laptop that contained the presentation. With your presentation in the cloud, you have no such worry. You can access it from your clients' computers in their offices or boardrooms with no possibility of losing anything in transit. As long as your client provides you with access to a web browser, that is.

When did you last attend a 'live' presentation anyhow? Haven't you noticed that many of the seminars that you would previously have attended in person have now been replaced with online 'webinars'? It makes sense if you want to reach an even wider international audience, and in this context the ability to embed a Google Docs presentation in a web page is one of the most useful features. Just choose **Publish / embed** from the **Share** menu like I have done in this Blogger blog:

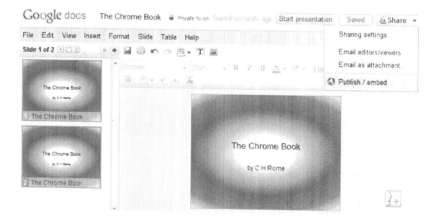

Once you have published the presentation to a unique web address URL for *all* to see (so beware) you can copy the embedding code that

begins "`<iframe src=`" into your Blogger blog or other web site so as to embed the presentation like this:

If you ever want to make the presentation unavailable, you can always click the **Stop publishing** button on the **Publish / embed** page.

Spreadsheet

Whereas the Google Docs 'Document' offering is a little restricting for my very exacting needs, I have found that the Spreadsheet offering more than lives up to what I would expect a spreadsheet program to do. It allows you to use formulas, functions, and cell references and retains most, if not all of these when converting to and from Microsoft Excel (.xls) format.

The spreadsheet shown below is one that I created as an example that may be useful to financial traders who hope to re-enter a stock position at a lower price than the price at which they last sold.

	Symbol	Price	Last Stop-Out	Want to...	Change Since Stop	%Change Since Stop	Open Signal	%Change Today	Info & Chart
24	HAS.L	111.048	107.74	Long	3.31	3.07%		-1.64%	http://uk.financ
25	HDY.L	208.4	216	Long	-7.60	-3.52%	3.52%	0.29%	http://uk.financ
27	HSD.L	157	160	Long	-3.00	-1.86%		-1.63%	http://uk.financ
28	INCH.L	377.8	299	Long	78.80	26.35%		-3.60%	http://uk.financ
29	IFL.L	20	19	Long	1.00	5.26%		1.27%	http://uk.financ
30	IPR.L	317.3	335	Long	-17.70	-5.28%	5.25%	-2.28%	http://uk.financ
31	IPO.L	49.5	29	Long	20.50	70.69%		3.13%	http://uk.financ
32	IPF.L	353.2	238	Long	115.20	48.40%		-3.42%	http://uk.financ
33	ITV.L	69.7	49	Long	20.70	42.24%		-1.48%	http://uk.financ
34	JJB.L	25	35	Long	-10.00	-26.57%	26.57%	-1.96%	http://uk.financ
35	JKX.L	288.7	285	Long	3.70	1.30%		-1.37%	http://uk.financ

The problem that this spreadsheet solves is not as important as the techniques it utilizes.

The user is able to enter a **Stock Symbol** in the first column, and this cell entry is used to fetch live data from the world wide web using the following formula:

=ImportData("http://download.finance.yahoo.com/d/quotes.csv?f=sl
1d1t1c1ohgv&e=.csv&s="&$A26)

This is pretty powerful stuff, which replicates the Microsoft Excel capability for retrieving web data using a Web Query.

The live price retrieved into the second column is compared with the user-entered **Last Stop-Out** (i.e. last selling price) in the third column so as to calculate and color-code the % **Change** in the sixth column. This demonstrates the ability to apply conditional formatting to cell contents.

In the final **Info & Chart** column, the user-entered **Stock Symbol** has been formulated into a web address URL that links to the stock's chart on the Yahoo! Finance web site (sorry Google!) thus demonstrating the spreadsheet string manipulation functions.

This is just one example, and I have presented it to show that it really is possible to do with the Google Docs spreadsheet pretty much all of the things you would have done with Microsoft Excel. This includes the ability to produce charts from your data as illustrated below, and with Google Docs you are able to publish your chart to a unique web address URL by clicking the **Publish chart** button that you can see in the picture.

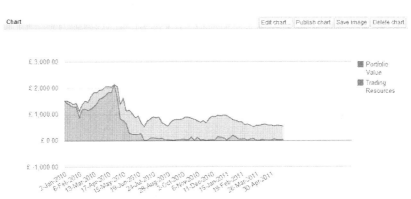

Form

You can use Google Docs to create a Form that you can embed in your web site or blog to collect information from your visitors. The figure below shows a form that I created so that, in the run up to this book's release, my blog visitors could sign up to be notified as soon as the book became available. It's a simple form with only one text box for user input, but I can tell you that it is also possible to include pick lists and choice buttons in the forms you create.

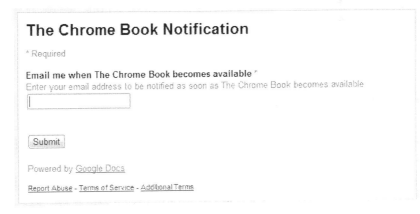

Each form that you create has a complementary spreadsheet, which is populated with a new entry each time a visitor submits your form; as illustrated below.

	A	B
1	**Timestamp**	**Email me when The Chrome Book becomes available**
2	5/14/2011 7:02:39	@yahoo.co.uk
3	5/14/2011 7:02:59	@yahoo.co.uk

This basic form functionality will be most suited to those of you who want to add an element of interactivity to your web site or blog without learning the necessary HTML code or other web programming techniques. One specific application for which I have found a Google Docs form to be most useful is in the provision of a web site 'contact me' form as an alternative to displaying an email address for all (including 'spammers') to see.

Drawing

As described in an earlier chapter, the Chromebook has a basic image editor that allows you to manipulate a picture by cropping, changing the brightness, or rotating it. But what if you want to further manipulate the picture? Maybe you want to annotate it, or combine several such pictures into one. Maybe you want to create a brand new picture from scratch. In other words, you might want to do the things that you used to do with Microsoft Paint, which is where the Google Docs Drawing application comes in handy.

You can start a new drawing by choosing **Drawing** from the **Create new** pull-down menu in Google Docs.

One of my biggest criticisms about Google Docs is that, as far as I can tell, it is difficult if not impossible to specify explicitly the exact *page size* of the documents, presentations and drawings that you create. As a book publisher this presents me with a problem, because I'd quite like to create my books' front and back covers as Google Docs drawings.

I need my book cover images to be exactly 6" wide by 9" tall with a resolution of 300 DPI (dots or pixels per inch) which would necessitate a drawing canvas size of 1800 x 2700 pixels. The first problem is that since Google Docs places a limit of 2000 x 2000 pixels on the drawings we create, I'll have to settle for 1334 x 2000 pixels to give a 6" x 9" result at a lower quality 221 DPI.

The second problem is that there appears to be no mechanism for specifying the exact dimensions of the drawing surface. A handle is provided at the bottom-right of the canvas, which you can drag horizontally and vertically to your required size... if you can guess where to position it! So I resorted to making the canvas as big as it would go, and then repeatedly dragging in the width and downloading the result as a JPG image -- using the **Download as** option from the **File** menu -- to see what dimensions I ended up with. Eventually, I achieved a downloaded image size of 1334 x 2000 pixels, so I named my drawing "6 x 9 Book Cover Template" and immediately used the **Make a copy** menu option so as to keep my correctly sized template pristine for future use. The purpose of this example is to show that you can usually achieve what you want to achieve using Google Docs, albeit sometimes via a roundabout route.

In the copy of my drawing, which I renamed as "Chrome Book Front Cover", I had a go at using the drawing tools to create my book's front cover. In the figure below you can see the drawing session in which I used a combination of shapes, word art, and text boxes to layout the cover. Notice how I centered the concentric circles outside of the canvas areas so that the image would crop to the centers of the circles at the bottom-right of the front cover.

By the time you read this book the cover may have changed again, because I'm rather fickle like that. In fact, it may have changed as a result of feedback from one of my collaborators, which leads us nicely to the Google Docs collaboration features.

Sharing

Any Google Docs document, spreadsheet, presentation, or drawing can be shared with others by choosing one of the options from the **Share** pull-down menu as shown below. You can also share any item within a collection, or an entire collection, by clicking the item in the Google Docs browser (not shown) and choosing the **Share** option from the pull-down menu of **Actions**.

Your sharing options are as follows.

Sharing settings...

Sharing settings allow you to make an item **Private** so that only you and those people that you specify can access it (if they sign in to Google Docs) as shown below. Alternatively, you can make an item available to **Anyone with the link** (if you tell them the specific web address URL of the item) or you can make it **Public to the Web** so that it shows up in web searches. In all three cases you can decide whether those who have access can edit the item or merely view it.

Sharing settings

Permissions:

🔒 Private - Only the people listed below can access   Change

👤 ⬛⬛⬛⬛⬛ (you)   Is owner

👤 LOTONtech Limited   Can edit ▼   ✕

Add people:

Enter names, email addresses, or groups...

Editors will be allowed to add people and change the permissions. [Change]

Close

Those people who you have deemed to be editors can post comments to your document as well as making changes to its content. Every posted comment is emailed to the document owner, and whenever the owner resolves a comment an email is sent to the editor who posted the comment. This can be both a blessing and a curse, as it can soon clog up your Inbox during an extensive reviewing and editing cycle.

Email editors/viewers...

Where you have entered a specific list of collaborators for a **Private item**, as shown above, you can **Email editors/viewers** (see last-but-one figure) with a message that also contains a link to the item.

Email as attachment...

In some cases you won't want to send out a hyperlink to the live item, but instead you will want to email a copy of the item as an attachment in a specific format like Microsoft Word (.doc) format. I would do this when submitting a written article to a magazine editor, by choosing the **Email as attachment** option. It's exactly like emailing a document or other file as an attachment as you would usually do, but now you're attaching it straight from the cloud and emailing it using your Gmail email address. This is important because you are not using valuable bandwidth by downloading the file over the Internet to your own computer or Chromebook simply to send it out again over the Internet.

Publish to the Web...

Regardless of your **Share settings**, you can choose any file to **Publish to the Web**. A copy of the file will be published with a unique web address URL, and this copy can be refreshed (optionally) when changes are made to the original. Thus you might provide the general public with temporary access to a copy of your file without giving away the location of the original, and you are able to un-publish the copy whenever you like.

Google Docs Advantages

Now you have some idea of how Google Docs works and what you can do with it. But why would you want to use it? What does Google Docs give you that your PC office suite doesn't? Here are some suggestions:

- Your open documents are saved automatically at regular intervals, so you don't have to become obsessive-compulsive about pressing the CTRL-S keyboard combination every few minutes in case your PC crashes. Yes, I have suffered in the past from CTRL-S obsessive-compulsive disorder... and for very good reason.
- Your stored documents have a complete revision history. If you make a mistake, you can rollback to a previous version by choosing **See revision history** from the Google Docs **File** menu.
- Since your documents are stored online in the cloud (i.e. on a Google server computer) you can access them from any computer anywhere via a web browser.
- You can easily share your documents with viewers and collaborators without resorting to sending them as email attachments.

Here's the most compelling reason for making the move to Google Docs rather than upgrading to the next version of your PC office suite:

It's free! (at least for individuals)

Google Docs Disadvantages

The main disadvantage of using Google Docs is that you have to be online to use it. You must be within range of a Wifi or 3G signal, you must be able to afford the data you are sending and receiving, and you are dependent on the performance of Google's server computers at the other end of your cloud connection. Personally, this is not a problem for me because most days I am connected to my 'all you can eat data' home / office broadband via Wifi. My fixed-line broadband deal grants me free access to thousands of FON Wifi hot spots (if I can find them!) while I'm out and about, and there are plenty of restaurants and bars that provide complimentary Wifi access to paying customers. If all else fails, I can get online via 3G as long as I can get a phone signal.

Note that since the first edition of this book it has become less essential for your Chromebook to be connected to the Internet 100% of the time. You can create and edit Google Docs documents off-line, but at the time of writing this applies only to the Document file type and not the Spreadsheet which is view-only in offline mode.

The other disadvantage is that, for some people, the functionality is currently simply not up to the standard set by PC-based office packages like Microsoft Office and Open Office. For most of you, this won't be a problem and it costs you nothing to find out by taking Google Docs for a spin.

Alternatives to Google Docs

Since Chrome is merely a web browser running on your PC, Chromebook or Chromebox, you are not restricted to using Google Docs on your Google Drive as your online office suite.

For some time I was a fan of the Adobe Buzzword online word processor that never really caught on; and for something rather more mainstream you might try the Microsoft Office online apps – including online versions of Word and Excel – that are accessible via the Microsoft SkyDrive (which is more-or-less the Microsoft equivalent of the Google Drive.

Depending on your needs, you might also find some handy third party office apps in the Chrome Web Store.

Summary

In this chapter I have described the various Google-format "office" files that you can create on your online Google Drive: Document, Presentation, Spreadsheet, Form and Drawing. I have introduced the idea of sharing your work and collaborating online, and I rounded off by suggesting some advantages and disadvantages of these tools while also reminding you that there are alternatives.

5 – Gmail, Contacts and Calendar

The Google Docs suite of applications discussed in the previous chapter is only half the story when it comes to using the Chrome web browser as the window on your cloud-based "office". Besides creating and editing documents of various kinds, you may also want to manage your personal or business email, contacts and calendar.

Gmail

When you initiate the Gmail application via its shortcut – or by typing **mail.google.com** into your web browser's address bar – you will notice at the top of the browser page, a ribbon of links to various Google apps like this:

Search Images Maps Play YouTube News **Gmail** Drive Calendar More ·

If you're not already using Gmail, the chances are good that you're using another web-based email provider like Yahoo! Mail or Hotmail. While it is possible to continue using these providers, and there is even a Yahoo! Mail App for Chrome,you might like to consider migrating to Gmail so that Google becomes your one-stop-shop with a single sign-in for email, calendar (discussed next) and documents (next chapter) on your PC, Chromebook and Android mobile phone. If you like the sound of it, you'll need some help with migrating to Gmail.

Migrating to Gmail

You already have a Google Account, so you already have a Gmail address which will be *yourgoogleaccountname@gmail.com*. What you don't yet have is access to the messages still flowing into your old email address; the messages you will need to see until you have notified all of your contacts that you have changed your email address. And what you don't yet know, which may be different from how your existing email interface works, is how to arrange your Gmail messages into a folder-like structure using labels. Let's look at each of these aspects in turn.

First, let's look at channeling messages from your old email address through to the Gmail interface. You don't have to do this because you could simply keep logging into your old email account to check for new messages, but I think it helps with the transition if you move decisively to Gmail as your single email application.

There are two ways in which you can channel incoming email messages from your old provider to Gmail. The first way is to forward the incoming messages, which I can demonstrate using the Yahoo! Mail **POP & Forwarding** options shown below. Notice that I have checked the option to **Forward your (BT) Yahoo! Mail** and I have entered my new Gmail email address.

The forwarding technique allows your old email provider to *push* incoming messages into your Gmail account. The other technique is for Gmail to *pull* the incoming messages from your old account, the key to which is also contained in the figure above. Notice how I could have checked the option to **Allow your (BT) Yahoo! Mail to be POPed** instead, in which case I would also need to do something in my Gmail account so as to actually do the *POPing*.

Clicking the small cog wheel ✿ at the top-right of your Gmail screen initiates a pull-down menu from which you can select the option to adjust your **Mail Settings**. On the **Mail Settings** page you can select the **Accounts** tab in order to set up one or more Post Office Protocol (POP) accounts within the **Get mail from other accounts** section of the page as shown below.

Get mail from other accounts:
(Download mail using POP3)
Learn more

@gmail.com
Last checked: 37 minutes ago. View history Check mail now

@btinternet.com
Last checked: 40 minutes ago. View history Check mail now

@btinternet.com
Last checked: 13 minutes ago. One mail fetched. View history Check mail now

Add a mail account you own

You can see that the 'old' email accounts that you set up for POPing are checked periodically, and you can set up a new one by clicking the link labeled **Add a mail account you own**. You will be guided through the setup process which will ask for your old email address (from which the correct settings will be determined automatically) and will send an email to your old address containing a verification code that you will need to enter in order to complete the process. In case you haven't figured it out, the verification step is to ensure that you really do own the old email account and that you are not fetching someone else's private correspondence into your Inbox.

On the subject of your Inbox; this is where any new emails to your old email address will now appear unless you decide to 'label' them as part of the setup process. This brings us nicely to the concept of labeling your email messages.

Labeling Email Messages

Many web-based email providers allow you to move messages from your **Inbox** into specific folders. Gmail allows you to do a similar thing by labeling your messages as shown below. You can see in this example how I have applied the **Personal** and **Work** labels to three of the messages in my **Inbox** using the **Labels** drop-down menu. You can also see how I could **Create new** labels and **Manage labels**.

It is possible to nest labels within labels so as to create a hierarchy (how about **Personal / 2010** and **Personal / 2011** and so on?) and you should have figured out from my example that any message can be given more than one label. By selecting the **Personal** label (in the far left column) I will be able to filter all messages labeled **Personal**, for example, regardless of which other labels are applied to those messages.

So I can label my messages, but they are still clogging up my Inbox, aren't they? I can move them out of the Inbox using the **Move to** drop-down menu that you can see in the above figure. Although the effect is similar to moving a message *to* a new or existing label, I think that this particular option might be better named **Move from**, because it disconnects the message from whichever labeled folder you are viewing and moves it to the new or existing label while retaining all other labels. So in my example, the effect of moving my already-labeled messages to the **Travel** label would be to remove the **Inbox** label while retaining the existing **Personal** and **Work** labels in addition to the new **Travel** label. So I didn't so much move the message *to* Travel as move it *from* the **Inbox**.

Contacts

Aren't you just sick of typing all your contacts into your mobile phone and then having to re-type them when you change phones? For the more technical readers: aren't you sick of syncing the contacts between your web-mail provider, the email application on your PC, and your mobile phone, only to find that some have gone missing in transit or have had their 'home' and 'mobile' numbers mysteriously switched around?

Let's keep it really simple then, by using your Google contacts list as the central repository for all your contacts. Watch how they magically get synced with the Contacts application on your Android mobile phone... and never get lost. Watch how there is no third contacts list stored on your PC, because your Chromebook simply accesses the contacts list in the Gmail web app via the Chrome browser.

You can access the Gmail contacts application by clicking the **Contacts** link that you can see at the top-left of the previous figure.

To get you off to a flying start, why don't you import your existing contacts, once only, from your Yahoo! Mail or Microsoft Outlook by choosing **Import** from the drop-down menu of **More actions**? You will need to have used the export function of your previous email / contacts program first.

Gmail Offline

As a further step towards making Chromebooks useable when not connected to the internet, Google offers a Gmail Offline application that is available in the Chrome Web Store. Although this app runs within a browser window, it provides a user interface not unlike traditional email clients like Microsoft Outlook (from what I remember) with the ability to read and compose messages when no internet connection is available.

Google Calendar

All good Personal Information Management (PIM) software such as Microsoft Outlook, every good web-based email provider, and all good mobile phone operating systems offer a calendar application to complement the *email* and *contacts* applications. Google provides a popular calendar application that you can access in at least three ways: either type **calendar.google.com** into your web browser's address bar, or click the application shortcut (if you've installed the web app), or click the link displayed in the ribbon at the top of your Gmail session:

Google Calendar provides all of the calendar functionality you are likely to need. You can set up multiple calendars; maybe one for business, and one for personal appointments. You can invite your friends or colleagues to events that you schedule in your calendar, and you can even access your friends' calendars (if they let you). You can view calendars by day, week, or month, and you can subscribe to calendar feeds from other calendars such as the **UK Holidays** calendar feed as shown below.

If you have an Android mobile phone, your Google Calendar can be automatically kept in sync with the **Calendar** app on your phone without ever having to connect up to a PC. And, if you're migrating to Google Calendar from another calendar application you will be pleased to know that you won't have to re-type all of your existing entries. Just click the **Add** link that you can see at the bottom-left of the previous figure, and browse for an **iCal** or **CSV** file that you have exported from Microsoft Outlook, Yahoo! Calendar, or whichever calendar application you used previously.

Don't forget that because the Google Calendar is entirely web based, you can access your calendar from any computer anywhere as long as it has a web browser.

Synchronized with Android

One of the most useful features of the Google mail, contacts and calendar suite is that it synchronizes automatically with those same apps on your Android mobile phone – providing you use the same Google Account on each device. Enter a new contact or calendar entry via your PC, Chromebook, or Android phone and see it synced automatically on all the other devices. Gone are the days when you had to do a three-way-sync between your mobile phone, Microsoft Outlook running on your PC, and your online email or calendar provided by Yahoo! or Google—so no more important meetings or contacts need go astray.

Summary

For many readers, the first experience of Google (apart from web searching) will have been through Google Mail (Gmail), the associated Contacts function and Calendar. For those of you in this position, the chapter you just read may well have alerted you to (or reminded you of) some of the less-obvious features that are at your disposal. For those of you who are not already using these facilities, isn't it about time you made the move?

the chrome book

6 – Google Apps (in Brief)

The greater part of this book is focused on the single user or family member who has bought a Chromebook and has signed up for a Google Account for personal use. This is only part of the Chromebook story, because Google also intends – or at least intended – for Chromebooks to appeal also to corporate clients due to their implicit reduced IT support costs; by which I mean that they are less likely to be adversely affected by user-installed software... and viruses.

Corporate clients will likely be interested in providing their staff with Chromebooks complemented by the more commercially-oriented Google Apps accounts; and that is the subject of this chapter. It's a relatively short (and optional) chapter because this book is still mainly about Google's Chromebook, Chrome web browser and cloud computing ecosystem as seen from the consumers' perspective.

Who Needs Google Apps?

Some companies will have adopted the Google cloud computing model by signing up with Google Apps and (optionally) by equipping their staff with easy-maintenance Chromebooks as an alternative to high-maintenance PCs. It may be via this route that you got your Chromebook and / or started using Google's web-based alternatives to the software programs you were used to. Or it may be that you have your own small business and you want to equip your staff with email addresses, communal calendar facilities, basic office functions, and simple devices (i.e. Chromebooks) to access those facilities without the need for an expensive IT department overhead.

Signing Up for Google Apps

There are at least two ways that I know of for signing up with Google Apps for your commercial enterprise:

1. Visit the web page at apps.google.com and **Start Free Trial** (if it's still available).

2. Apply for a Google-arranged custom domain for your Blogger blog (see screenshot below) and get Google Apps thrown in for your new domain.

Publishing

Blog Address   thechromebook.blogspot.com   will redirect to your domain

Buy a domain for your blog

http://www   thechromebook   .com

Domains are registered through a Google partner and cost $10 (USD) for one year. As part of registration, you will also get a Google Apps account for your new domain.

What You Get with Google Apps

Google Apps allows you as a business owner to provide your staff with a complete set of office tools through which they can collaborate online. The current lineup of tools includes Gmail, Calendar, Drive (incorporating Docs, Sheets, and Slides), Sites (which is rather like Microsoft SharePoint as far as I can tell), and Vault (for audited archiving).

Note that the emphasis is on online storage (so that all data is automatically backed up) and collaboration (so that users can easily arrange meetings and work on the same documents at the same time).

Managing Multiple Users

Suppose you signed up with Google Apps as a new company called LOTONtech Limited. Well, you might not, but I would. And if I did, I would likely create a new user account for the pseudo-named author of this book (C H Rome) as shown below.

This new user could henceforth sign in to a Chromebook or Chromebox, or a PC running the Chrome web browser using the email address that was allocated. He could also sign in via another web browser using the company-specific web address http://www.google.com/a/lotontechlimited.com.

Although each user's experience of Gmail, Google Drive and so on would be pretty much the same as the individual user experience described throughout this book, I (as the business owner) would be able to manage these users by assigning them specific privileges and allocating them to groups.

Summary

The purpose of this chapter has been to highlight the fact that even a modest enterprise can establish a multi-user enterprise-wide IT infrastructure … without the IT infrastructure. All thanks to cloud computing.

7 – The Chrome Web Store

Just as the Apple iPad has its iTunes web store, and just as Android phones have the Android Market, so Chrome has the Chrome Web Store from where you can install *web apps*. These web apps, which are mostly just packaged web sites rather than installable programs, are not necessarily Chromebook-specific and can be utilized just as effectively when running via the Chrome web browser on your traditional PC.

The Web Store also offers a large number of Chrome browser extensions, which act more like installable utility programs or browser plug-ins. These extensions might perform local tasks – like interacting with your computer hardware – which remotely running web apps cannot perform.

You can visit the Chrome Web Store by clicking the app icon of that name or by typing https://chrome.google.com/webstore into the Chrome browser's address bar. In the following picture I have launched the web store and drilled down into the **Dictionaries** sub-category of the **Utilities** category. You can also find the apps by searching the store.

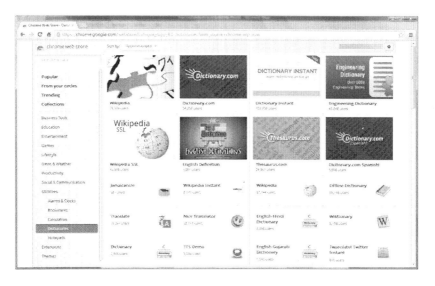

Apps vs. Extensions (and Packaged Apps)

I've already hinted that there is a difference between *apps* (which are glorified web sites) and *extensions* (which are locally-installed programs rather like browser plug-ins). It used to be that the Chrome Web Store made an explicit distinction between Apps and Extensions, but now the distinction is less obvious.

Perhaps the best way to understand the difference between apps and extensions is to think of apps as distinct browser destinations that provide specific functionality – like editing documents or checking the financial news – whereas extensions enhance the features of the Chrome web browser *across apps and web sites*. So for example, you might install the **ChromeVox** extension that allows the web browser to speak the content of any web site that you visit.

I have to admit that I became weary of the ChromeVox constant chatter after a while; in which context you will be pleased to know that it is easy to disable or even remove specific browser extensions via the **Extensions** category of the **Chrome Settings**. Like this:

For completeness, I should tell you that there is a third class of installable component that blurs the boundary between web apps and extensions; this is the *packaged app*. While *web apps* (also known as *hosted apps*) are basically wrappers for existing web sites, *packaged apps* are downloaded and locally-installed apps that can function even when the user is offline. The latter are similar to the "apps" that you are used to installing on your mobile phone.

Personally I think that the introduction of packaged apps goes against the original spirit of the Chrome OS providing lightweight web access as a pure thin client. With these installable apps and the PC-like desktop the Chromebook is looking and behaving more and more like a traditional PC all the time, which of course may be necessary in order to attract more converts. It's also beginning to look more and more like the Android operating system that provides a desktop of sorts along with a suite of installable apps, and a web browser — and this may be no accident because Google is known to be considering merging its two operating systems (Chrome OS and Android) in the future.

Themes

In addition to apps and extensions, the Chrome Web Store also offers browser **Themes**. These made perfect sense in the early days when the Chrome web browser occupied the whole of the Chromebook screen, but are not so compelling now that Chromebooks have a PC-style "desktop" that is unaffected by these in-browser themes. Still, they provide a way to add a little sparkle to your browsing session —

for example by installing the metallic "Brushed" theme as shown below.

In the following screenshot I have killed two birds with one stone by showing what another Chrome theme looks like while also demonstrating an additional Chromebook feature: the ability to perform rudimentary image manipulations – in this case cropping – on any images you open on the Chromebook.

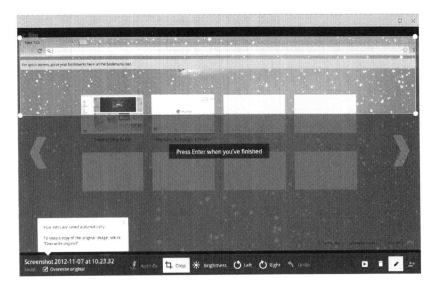

Not Just for Chromebooks and Chromeboxes

The Chrome Web Store is not only home to apps, extensions and themes for your Chromebook or Chromebox, but also home to apps and extensions for the Chrome web browser running on your PC—if you still have one.

Summary

Just as most mobile phones have their respective online stores for media and apps, so the Chrome web browser has its own Chrome Web Store for hosted apps, packaged apps, extensions and themes.

8 – The Chrome Web Browser

Since the Chrome web browser preceded the Chrome OS and Chromebook computer by a few years, there are already several books that will tell you in detail how this web browser works. You may already have read one of these books, or maybe you've used the Chrome browser already on your 'legacy' PC. In any event, you will no doubt have used one of the other browsers like Internet Explorer or Mozilla Firefox that do essentially the same job. What is important here then, is to present the features of the Chrome browser that distinguish it from all the other web browsers when it is running on a Chromebook computer.

Tabs and Windows

You are probably already familiar with the fact that the Chrome browser (just like most other web browsers) allows you to open separate web pages in separate browser tabs, and I told you as much in an earlier chapter. This ability to open web pages in separate tabs within a single browser window was a great advance when first introduced to PC web browsers, because it saved you from launching the web browser program multiple times. Nevertheless, it is sometimes useful to have entirely separate browser sessions running, with different arrangements of tabs in each one, so that (for example) you can open all your email message tabs in one window and all your document tabs in another window. For this reason, the Chrome OS allows you to launch separate browser windows and switch between them using the dedicated keyboard key (shown again below) on your Chromebook. Pressing it multiple times will cycle through your various browser windows.

Bringing the two ideas together, you will be interested to know that you can "tear off" a browser tab to become a separate browser window; as in the following screenshot where I am in the process of tearing the Google Drive tab from my Google Calendar browser window so that it becomes a browser window in its own right.

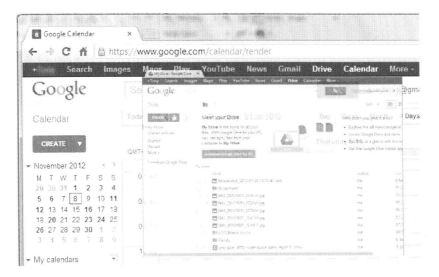

Bookmarks

In the **Customize and Control** menu that you can access by clicking the icon at the top-right of the Chrome browser (see below) you will see a menu option titled **Bookmark manager**, and in the Tools sub-menu you will see an option to **Always show bookmarks bar**.

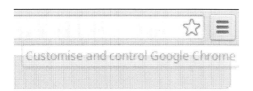

Just as in any web browser, you can bookmark your favorite web pages so that you can launch them at the click of a mouse... or tap of the touchpad. You can add a bookmark for the web page you are currently viewing by clicking the star to the right of the browser address bar.

Where it gets really interesting with the Chrome web browser is when you are signed in to your Chromebook or when you "sign in" to the Chrome web browser itself (which is not the same thing as simply signing into your Google Account) on your PC as shown below.

Your bookmarks and browsing history will now follow you to any device on which you sign into Chrome.

Settings

You can access your Chrome browser settings either by selecting **Settings** from the pull-down menu as shown below, or by typing **chrome://chrome/settings** into the browser address bar, or (on a Chromebook) by clicking your user picture at the bottom-right of the screen and selecting **Settings**.

The settings that you see and can configure will depend on whether you're running the Chrome browser on a PC or on a Chromebook / Chromebox. On a Chromebook these settings refer to your settings on the actual device, so in this case they will include such things as **Internet connection** and **Touchpad speed**.

Some of the more interesting settings can be found by clicking the **Show advanced settings** link at the foot of the settings page. For example, the settings for the Google Cloud Print facility that is described in *Chapter 10 – Cloud Computing Conundrums*. When running the Chrome web browser on a Chromebook you will find a **Factory Reset** option, which may be useful when you decide to sell on your Chromebook (why would you?). Otherwise, be careful with this option; but with all of your data stored on the cloud you should be relatively protected if your finger strays towards this "self-destruct" button!

Is the Web Browser really the Operating System?

In the first iterations of the Chromebook concept it could be said that the web browser was the computer's operating system, because all user activity took place within the web browser. In more recent iterations, Google seems to have lost its nerve somewhat with the "everything within the browser" paradigm and has introduced a more PC-like desktop. Nonetheless, the Chrome web browser is very much the centerpiece for the Chromebook user experience — even for locally installable "offline" apps.

If we ignore the fact that the Chromebook client operating system is actually based on Linux (which is largely invisible), standardization of the user experience within the browser has allowed Google to extend the Chrome OS experience across traditional PCs and other devices in addition to dedicated Chromebook and Chromebox devices.

This is only half the story as far as the computer operating system is concerned. The fact is that computer operating systems have essentially two parts: the *interaction part* and the *execution part*:

- The *interaction part* of the operating system comprises what you see on the screen (traditionally the Windows desktop) and how you interact with the computer using a keyboard, mouse, web cam, or some externally-connected peripheral such as a scanner.
- The *execution part* is the part of the operating system that allows you to install programs and keep them running.

Whereas the Chrome web browser and the underlying lightweight Linux-based Chrome OS operating system present you with the *interaction part* of the operating system, the *execution part* of the operating system is not necessarily running on your computer at all. This is the world of cloud computing, where when you edit a Google Docs document most of the heavy lifting – i.e. 'running the program' – takes place on Google's own remote server computers.

The computer in front of you may be simply taking your input via keyboard and track-pad, instructing the Google server to crunch your numbers, and then presenting your results in the browser window. It's just like in the old days of mainframe computers and green screen terminals... but now with more colors.

Summary

In this chapter I have summarized some of the key features of the Chrome web browser: its tabs and windows, bookmarks (which can be synchronized across devices) and settings. I have also emphasized the fact that the Chrome web browser constitutes pretty much the entire operating environment of the Chromebook computer... at least from the user's perspective.

9 – Your Google Account

The common thread that runs through your Gmail, Google Docs, Blogger (if you use it) and other Google services is your Google Account.

When you first set up your Chromebook computer you will have been obliged to create at least one Google account, or to log in to a Google account that you already owned. If you own an Android mobile phone you may already have discovered that you can make best use of your phone by associating it with a new or existing Google account. If you've ever created a blog using Blogger, or used Google Adsense or Adwords, you will have a Google account.

However your Google account came about, you will want to manage it, which you can do by visiting the web page at https://www.google.com/accounts/ManageAccount or by choosing the **Account settings** link from the pull-down menu of options available by clicking your Gmail email address shown at the top-right of your browser pages when using any Google application.

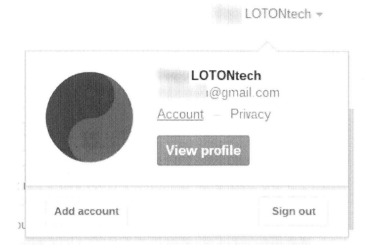

There are various things you can manage on an account, depending on whether it is a personal account or a company (staff) account set up for you by an organization via Google Apps. In this chapter I focus on just two areas that I consider to be the most important: Security and Storage.

Security

The most important thing you will do in your Google account is to manage your password. Since your Gmail address and password combination is the key to everything stored in your Google cloud, it is important that you remember it while at the same time not making it obvious and guessable.

Fortunately, you are provided with a couple of mechanisms for recovering your password in the event that you forget what it is. You can record an alternative **recovery email address** to which a password reminder can be sent, and you can specify a security question such as "What is the name of your best friend from childhood?" that you will be asked in the event that you wish to reset your password.

Note that if ever you change your Google password – which perhaps you should do periodically – you will have to update any client devices that sign into your Google account. For example, the Gmail application on your Android mobile phone will prompt for your password when it finds that a connection cannot be made using your old password.

Storage

At the time of writing, Google provides limited cloud storage of 5GB for new account holders. If you bought one of the October 2012 Samsung Chromebooks it is likely that you were offered 100GB of online storage for two years when you first access the **Files** app on the device. At the time of writing it is worth $5-per-month, therefore $120 in total. Not bad, but do keep in mind that if you fill most or all of the storage during the two years then you will have to commit to the prevailing rate for that level of storage once the offer period has ended. Don't worry, you won't lose any of your files, but you won't be able to store new files on the cloud once the offer period has concluded unless you sign up for a storage plan.

Whatever your storage starting point (I already had a paid-for plan in place), you can always pay by credit or debit card to increase your storage at https://www.google.com/settings.

While I'm not a big fan of paid-for services when so much functionality is available on the web for free, I do think that these fees are quite reasonable. If you're dead set on not paying for anything unless you really have to, you could theoretically increase your total storage to 20GB (for example) by creating four separate Google accounts with 5GB allocated to each one for free. Although these would be entirely separate storage accounts, the sharing features of Google Drive might be used to at least give the "illusion" of a single cloud storage area.

Note that any Google Docs format documents that you create do not count towards your storage usage, which I guess is one way for Google to encourage the use of their online office suite rather than the Microsoft alternative.

Multiple Google Accounts

I like to have at least two Google accounts, so that I can separate my personal and business activities and so that I can have different personal and business email addresses. Therefore, I sometimes need to log in to two different accounts simultaneously on the same Chromebook or another device.

On your **Account settings** page you will see an option to allow **Multiple sign-in**, which by default should be switched off. Clicking the link marked **Edit** will take you to the page shown below. You can use it to switch the **Multiple sign-in** feature **On** once you have read the various warnings; these warnings being there mainly to advise you that you may get confused and end up doing things in the wrong account.

Once you have enabled multiple sign-in you can switch between your accounts by pulling down the menu of options attached to your user name (i.e. yourname@gmail.com) at the top-right of your Gmail or Google Docs session.

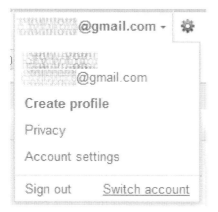

Choose the **Switch account** or **Sign in to another account** option (not shown) to switch to one of your other accounts, and see how it opens a new browser tab with your alternate identity.

Personally, I prefer to do this a slightly different way by opening a new browser window (click the wrench icon and choose **New window**) so that my two identities are kept completely separate in entirely different windows. Even better, when working on a traditional Windows PC I prefer to log into my two Google Accounts (personal and business) using two entirely different web browsers: Google Chrome, and Microsoft Internet Explorer respectively.

Multiple Accounts on Your Chromebook or Chromebox

What I just described is a necessary way of "switching context" between Google Accounts when running the Chrome web browser on a PC that takes an age to switch between real users. Since the Chromebook allows you to sign out of one account quite quickly via the initial sign-on screen, and since those separate user accounts are tied absolutely to particular Google Accounts in the Chrome web browser, I actually find it much easier – and less confusing – to switch between accounts in this way when operating a Chromebook.

Summary

Your Google Account is the linchpin that connects your settings and data across your Chrome browser sessions on different devices at different times. Via your Google Account you can set your security and storage preferences.

It is just about possible to utilize multiple Google accounts (different identities, if you have them) within a single Chrome browser session on your PC; but it is more effective to keep these accounts entirely separate by signing into your Chromebook as different users—which is both fast and effective.

the chrome book

10 – Cloud Computing Conundrums

The low-maintenance Chromebook and Chromebox computers, and the wider Google cloud computing model, present a set of conundrums: tasks that you used to be able to perform quite easily using your traditional PC, but which the cloud computing model makes more difficult. In this chapter I present some of those cloud computing conundrums, and (most helpfully) the potential solutions.

But first, let me start by stating that the Chrome OS *doesn't* at all present one of the conundrums presented by the comparative Apple devices such as the iPad. Many of the financial trading web sites and other web sites that I use daily require my computing device (laptop, phone or tablet) to run Adobe Flash content in the web browser. On the iPad and on other Apple iOS powered devices this is simply impossible, because those devices won't run Flash. The Chromebooks and Chromeboxes have no such limitation.

Okay, so much for what Chrome OS devices can do that the iPad can't. Now what about those things that Chromebooks, Chromeboxes and other Chrome OS devices struggle with?

Printing

The most obvious cloud computing problem is printing. Chromebooks were designed not to run locally-installed software, and this includes printer drivers, so there is little point trying to attach a printer to your Chromebook computer. Well, the "paperless office" has been a little slower in materializing than we might have hoped, and so most of us still need to print content as hard copy (i.e. on paper) from time to time.

This conundrum can be addressed in (at least) two ways:

HP ePrint

Since the printing problem is a problem for users of smart phones and tablets that don't generally allow you to attach printers, as well as for Chromebooks and Chromeboxes, Hewlett Packard came up with an ingenious solution in the form of its ePrint range of printers.

These printers connect up to HP's ePrint service on the Internet via your wireless router, and allow you to associate an email address with the printer. Printing on one of these printers from your Chromebook, phone or tablet – even from miles away – can be as simple as sending your document as an email attachment to:

emailaddressofmyprinter@hpeprint.com (not a real email address)

If the email address of your printer became widely known, anyone could print to it, although it's anyone's guess as to why they would want to. To inundate you with SPAM printer advertisements, I guess.

Rest assured that it is possible to configure the settings via the ePrint Center web site at https://h30495.www3.hp.com/ so that only recognized email addresses (the **Allowed Senders**) can send print jobs to your printer.

Google Cloud Print

On the HP ePrint Settings dialog just shown, you can see a third tab labeled **Print Services**, and here lies the second solution to the printing conundrum – in the form of **Google Cloud Print**.

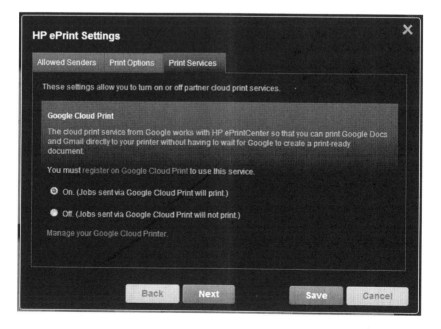

Once you've registered a printer with the Google Cloud Print Service – which means associating it with your Google Account – you can print to it as though the printer is attached to your Chromebook or Chromebox. You can see the **Google Cloud Print** dialog in the following screenshot, via which I have chosen to send a document from Gmail running on my Chromebook to a HP Photosmart printer that I had previously registered with Google Cloud Print.

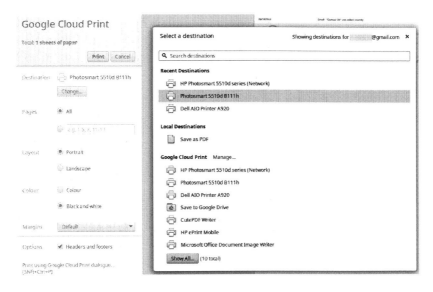

Note that alternatively you can **Save as PDF**, which enables you to store a "printed" copy of your content (in this case an email message) as an electronic Portable Document Format (PDF) file in your Chromebook's **Downloads** folder – from where you might copy it to your Google Drive for permanent safe keeping.

Note also that your connected printer need not be a HP printer, it might be a Canon or some other printer brand, and it need not be an e-printer at all… as I will now explain.

Connecting Your PC Printer to Google Cloud Print

When running the Chrome web browser on your traditional PC, the browser **Settings** (as shown below) should include a section titled **Google Cloud Print**. I already have some printers connected – therefore I can **Disconnect printers** – but *you* won't.

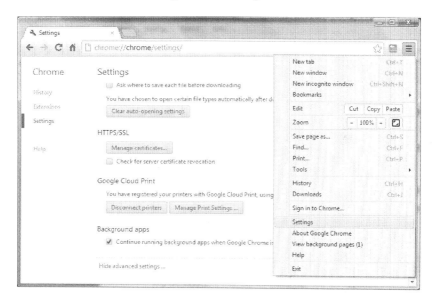

If you never did this before, you will have the option to **Add Printers**, and after signing into your Google Account you should find that any printer attached to your PC will be registered with the Cloud Print Service. It means that providing your PC is switched on and connected to the Internet, you can print to its attached printer from your Chromebook or Chromebox via Cloud Print. This is a useful interim solution for those people who continue to own legacy PC hardware (and printers) while transitioning to the world of cloud computing with Chrome.

Windows Programs via the Chrome Remote Desktop

I reckon I can exist 90% "in the cloud", simply interacting Google Apps and the other web sites I use on a regular basis. But as a book publisher I also do some pretty hardcore stuff using Microsoft Word.

Reconciling these two worlds – my desire to carry only a Chromebook with me wherever I go, and my need to access the advanced features of Microsoft Word – presents me with a problem. Or does it?

I have a perfectly serviceable desktop PC that runs Microsoft Word, and I have a broadband router that allows this desktop PC to be always connected to the Internet. If only there was away to somehow "dial in" to this PC from my Chromebook, and to interact with it via the Chromebook keyboard and screen (from wherever I happen to be at the time), then I wouldn't be limited by the fact that I can't run this Windows software directly on my Chromebook.

You won't be surprised to learn that I'm leading up to the fact that... you can do exactly what I just described, but using the Chrome Remote Desktop. Here's how...

On Your PC

First you need to do a little setup at the PC end.

Using the Chrome web browser, visit the Web Store at https://chrome.google.com/webstore and search for "chrome remote desktop". When you find the **Chrome Remote Desktop** app, click the button marked **ADD TO CHROME. ,** followed by the button to **LAUNCH APP.**

You will be prompted to select a Google Account, and then to **Allow Access.**

The remote desktop has a **Remote Assistance** option which is intended for technical support staff to gain temporary access to someone else's computer, and a **My Computers** option that allows you to access and operate your home or office-based PC remotely from your Chromebook.

Upon clicking the **Enable remote connections** button shown in the screenshot above, you will be prompted to enter a PIN that ensures only you can access your PC remotely. Once the remote desktop feature has been enabled, you should ensure that the PC (especially laptop) power settings are such that it will not go to sleep just when you really want to access it remotely.

On Your Chromebook

Once you've set up the PC end of the remote connection you can launch the Chrome Remote Desktop app on your Chromebook. You should see your PC listed in the **My Computers** section of the page as shown below, and you can simply click (and enter your PIN) to connect.

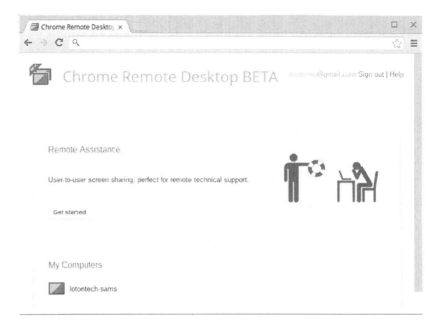

Everything you do on your PC screen will appear automatically on your Chromebook screen, and vice versa, which can be quite spooky. You can operate your PC from your Chromebook *as though it is your PC,* and can run all your favorite programs... even if you're in another room or another city. The following screenshot shows my Chrome Remote Desktop session running Microsoft Word, and I'm using it to edit the manuscript for the book you are reading now.

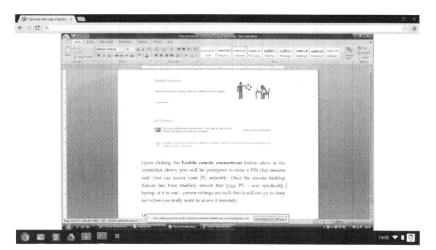

Here's a tip: it looks much better if you go full-screen in the Chrome browser so that your screen is filled with the contents of the PC screen. If you have another Chrome browser window running on your Chromebook, perhaps for your Gmail, you can easily switch between the "PC screen" and Chromebook screen(s) by pressing the "switch windows" key on the Chromebook keyboard.

The PC Feedback Loop

Since it is perfectly possible to run the Chrome Remote Desktop within the Chrome browser running on a PC, and to use it to connect up to exactly the same PC desktop, I thought it would be fun to see what would happen in this scenario. Sure enough you get a video feedback loop, with a screen within a screen within a screen and so on... ad infinitum. It was a bit of fun, and no doubt you'll be keen to try it, but it's not something I would recommend once the initial novelty has worn off.

Connecting via 3G on Your Mobile Phone

Some people prefer the convenience of a 3G-enabled Chromebook on which they can obtain an essential (for a Chromebook) Internet connection wherever they can get a mobile signal, although a Wifi connection would almost always be more cost-effective where available.

Some people are happy enough to opt for a cheaper Wifi-only Chromebook model and to rely solely on Wifi hotspots at home, at work, or in public places (like restaurants) for the essential Internet connection.

I'm in the latter camp because if I really need to connect my Chromebook to the Internet via 3G, I can do so using my Android mobile phone. It saves me from having separate mobile data contracts for my phone and my Chromebook, and – theoretically, at least – it means I can connect my Chromebook via the much-faster 4G mobile network in future by simply upgrading my phone and without having to upgrade my Chromebook.

I can achieve this feat by enabling my Android phone for USB Tethering or as a Portable Wifi Hotspot. For the record, the phone I am using to achieve this feat is a two-year-old Google / Samsung Nexus S phone running Android version 4.1.2 (it worked on some earlier versions) and connected to the UK's "3" mobile 3G network. You may or may not be able to achieve the same thing, depending on your phone and mobile carrier.

Tethering & portable hotspot

Within the **WIRELESS & NETWORKS** section of your Android phone's **Settings**, you should see an option labeled **Tethering and portable hotspot**. Selecting this option should present you with a number of options as shown in the following screenshot; options for **USB Tethering**, **Portable Wi-Fi hotspot**, and **Bluetooth tethering**.

The most straightforward option is the **USB tethering** option which will be grayed-out unless you have connected your phone to your Chromebook using a USB cable. Once you've connected the cable and enabled the option, you should see a new network named **Ethernet** on your Chromebook:

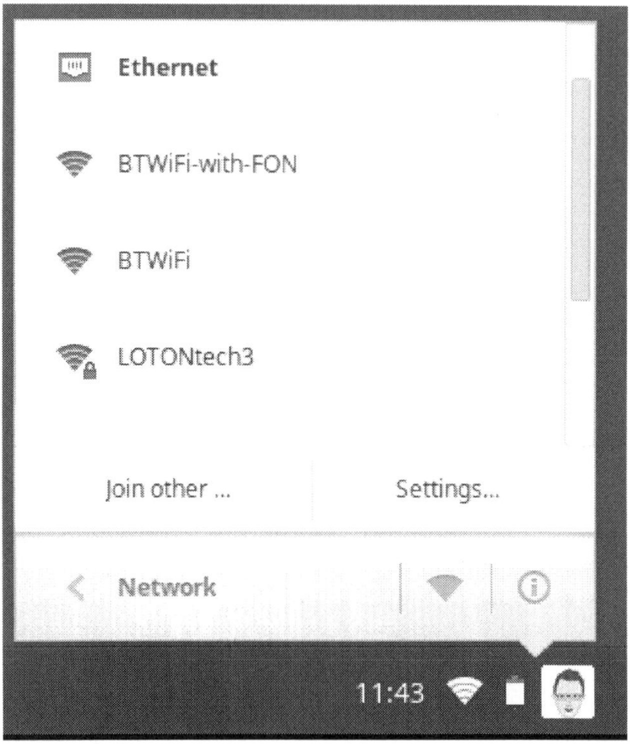

In the list of networks shown above, you can also see a network named **LOTONtech3**, which is a wireless network that became available when I enabled the **Portable Wi-Fi hotspot** option on my Android phone.

The final option is to tether your Android phone and your Chromebook together using the **Bluetooth tethering** option, but I'll leave that one for you to try yourself. I've never been a big fan of the additional "pairing" step that is required in order to get Bluetooth devices to play together.

Summary

The Chrome cloud computing model presents some interesting opportunities to work and play in ways that were simply not possible before; but is also presents some challenges such as how to print and how to run the (Windows) software programs that you used to know and love. So in the chapter I have addressed some of those cloud computing conundrums.

When it comes to one of the solutions in particular – the Chrome Remote Desktop – I use this feature rather more than I expected; for example when sitting on my bed (Chromebook on my lap) while the remotely-connected PC that I am interacting with is sitting in my office.

11 – My Head in the Clouds

In the first edition of this book I began this final chapter by stating that I had not (yet) fully moved to the cloud. That's still true, just about, but I'm moving closer all the time. The only real stumbling block is my hardcore use of Microsoft Word to typeset documents and manipulate images for publication; both for myself and for other people. But that's no longer such a valid excuse with the advent of the Chrome Remote Desktop that allows me to work with even my PC software via my Chromebook wherever I happen to be in the world — providing I keep just one PC, and keep it switched on and connected to the internet.

Otherwise, when doing my regular work of writing articles for online and print journals, all that the journal editors require is a simple free-flowing document in Microsoft Word (.doc) format with a basic header structure and a few embedded pictures. When it comes to writing for financial publications, I sometimes need to put together a spreadsheet or two. In all respects, Google Docs is up to the job and I need not come out of the cloud.

For everything else that I do – reading and responding to emails, reading the news, online banking, and so on – I had already existed almost exclusively within the cloud, albeit using a traditional (and frankly over-engineered) PC to run my web browser. Several years ago I switched from using an email client program like Microsoft

Outlook to accessing my emails only through a provider web site such as Gmail.

What finally prompted me to take up almost fulltime residence in the cloud was the fact that the screen on my Windows laptop computer flickered and died thereby rendering it my new 'desktop' computer with an external monitor plugged in. It wasn't much use to me on the road, and in the time taken to consider a repair or replacement I became ever-more-reliant on whichever of my family's or friends' computers or other web connected devices came to hand. However and wherever I logged in, I had almost instantaneous access to the important documents I was working on via Google Docs (now Google Drive). There was no need to worry about a catastrophic hard disk crash or whether I remembered to back up my data yesterday.

So here I am now, sitting on my bed writing this paragraph using Microsoft Word that is running on my remotely-connected laptop-turned-desktop PC via my Chromebook keyboard and screen. With one tap of the Chromebook "switch windows" key I'm checking my Gmail in the Chrome browser, and in a separate browser tab I'm updating an entry in my Google Calendar. Meanwhile I'm listening to a song which the Chromebook's built-in Audio Player found on my plugged-in USB stick and is playing in the background.

Google is Not the Only Cloud

In this book I have focused on cloud computing with Google hardware, software and services. But finally, I should remind you that Google is not the only cloud.

I have assumed, or at least suggested, that you will adopt the set of cloud computing solutions offered by Google: Gmail for your email, Google Docs (via Google Drive) as your office application suite, and so on. But Google is not the only cloud computing show in town.

I have already hinted that Adobe provides – or at least used to provide – an entirely web-based office suite at www.acrobat.com. Those of you with a Microsoft Live ID can create and store Word, PowerPoint, and Excel documents on your SkyDrive at skydrive.live.com. You might have so much investment in Microsoft Hotmail as your email provider that you're not quite ready to switch to Gmail just yet.

The good news is that the Chrome browser is simply a web browser, so – even when running on a Chromebook computer – it should allow you to use alternative cloud solutions as well as (or instead of) those provided by Google. Indeed, Google is more open than some providers to the prospect of you using the best third-party solutions for your needs, else why would they provide a Chrome Web Store populated with third-party solutions?

Having painted this rosy picture of every vendor coexisting in the cloud in peace and harmony, I should warn you that you will need to double-check that your alternative cloud computing suite really will run on your Chromebook + Chrome combo. Some Microsoft web sites may require or at least encourage you to install their Windows-dependent Silverlight browser extension. Even if your alternative cloud computing suites run faultlessly, you may need to think about how the various cloud computing solutions fit together. Want to reroute your incoming email messages from Hotmail or Yahoo! Mail to your Gmail Inbox, or reroute your incoming Gmail to one of the other providers? No problem at all. Want to write a document initially using Google Docs, and then download it in Microsoft Word (.doc) format for uploading to your Windows SkyDrive for further editing? No Problem. Want to go the other way? Well, it's not so easy because the Microsoft Office Web Apps are designed to be an adjunct to the fully paid-up Microsoft Office Suite—so they assume that you have Word installed locally on your PC even though you are using the web-based alternative.

In a nutshell: interoperability between cloud computing solutions should be possible, and with a little ingenuity and lateral thinking... it is. But, I have found that I can save myself a great deal of time and effort by wherever possible making Google my 'one stop shop' for cloud computing solutions.

When it comes to accessing my Google cloud, I don't have to do so from a Google device such as a Chromebook or Chromebox, even though I prefer to do so. I can access my Gmail and Google Docs from an Android mobile phone or tablet (okay, these are Google devices) or from a traditional Windows PC running the Chrome browser.

The choices are yours to make; but when all is said and done, for me, it's Google all the way.

C H Rome

In the unlikely event that you haven't figured out the reasoning behind the pseudonym, let me spell it out for you... literally. It's **CHRome**.

chromebook.lotontech.com

Index

20533460R00062

Made in the USA
Lexington, KY
10 February 2013